D0931793

CREEPY CHRONICLES

# Spooky Spirits and Creepy Creatures

Written by Barbara Cox and Scott Forbes

Gareth Stevens
Publishing

# CONTENTS

What's the scariest creature you can think of? Does it have a mouthful of sharp teeth, pointy claws, and a thirst for blood? Maybe a hideous troll, evil fairy, disgusting gremlin, or a giant ogre is the worst thing you can imagine?

From the murkiest swamps to the darkest skies and the driest deserts to the highest mountains, there are said to be dragons, goblins, giant birds, flying serpents, and monstrous lizards all over the world. Do these sinister creatures really exist or are they only in our imaginations? It doesn't matter since there's nowhere to hide. Just try not to think about it.

# SPOOKY SPIRITS AND CREEPY CREATURES

# EVIL FAIRY

**In general, the small supernatural beings known as fairies are good and friendly toward humans. But you can't trust them all.**

Some fairies have turned evil and will do all they can to cause terror and suffering. They place curses on people to make them sick or bring them bad luck. And they steal people's souls—even those of babies—and hide them away. In place of the stolen soul, they leave behind a "changeling," an evil or insane creature that will torment its new family. In Ireland and Scotland, where such fairies are common, people who seem troubled or distracted are often said to be "away with the fairies."

# IMP

**According to legend, Imps were among the followers of Satan, or the Devil, thrown out of Heaven by God.**

Since then, Imps have often found favor as servants of witches or wizards, though many wander alone. As demons go, Imps are usually small in size and more mischievous than evil. Nevertheless, they can be quite alarming in appearance, having thin, scaly, lizard-like bodies, pointy ears and noses, and bat-like wings. Some of their tricks can be quite unpleasant, too. Some of their favorites include tripping people so that they hurt themselves and tricking people into getting lost, especially in forests.

# GOBLIN

**GOBLINS ARE SMALL** supernatural creatures who pester, infuriate, and even terrorize humans. Descriptions of them vary, though they are usually said to be humanlike, child-sized or smaller, sometimes bald, and often green in color, with a pointed nose and ears and an almost constantly sly expression.

## LITTLE ROGUES

The word "goblin" comes from the Greek *kobalos*, meaning "rogue," and these little guys are certainly mischievous, as well as frequently frightening and sometimes downright evil. Normally they live in forest caves or tree hollows, but they often take up residence in houses, mainly with the aim of driving the human occupants mad. To achieve this, they steal things, make strange noises, move furniture around, clatter pots and pans, and knock on walls. So, if you hear any bumps in the night, it could very well be a goblin.

Some say that goblins emerged in the British Isles and then spread across Europe. But similar creatures have been known for centuries in many parts of the world, including India, China, and Japan. Particular kinds of goblins have also emerged within Europe, including the Kobolds of Germany, which create havoc in silver mines, and the Trows of Scotland's Orkney Islands, which live in earth mounds and sneak into houses at night to work their mischief.

Goblins are often very small, some no higher than an inch tall.

# HINKYPUNK

**THE HINKYPUNK, also known as Will o' the Wisp or Jack o'Lantern, is a marsh spirit whose treacherous light draws travelers to a swampy death.**

## BEWARE OF THE LIGHTS

Hinkypunks are found all over the world, wherever there are deserted and dangerous marshes, bogs, and swamps.

The Hinkypunk crosses the marsh, carrying a light which, from a distance, looks like a lantern or torch carried by a human traveler. People who are lost in the marsh follow the light in the hope of finding a way through, but the Hinkypunk leads them astray and they step into the deep watery mud, never to be seen again.

Hinkypunks go around the marshes alone or in groups—the groups are more dangerous, since they usually spread out along an apparent "path," and their lights look as if a row of people are walking through the swamp.

Some believe that a Hinkypunk only has one leg, on which it hops nimbly. This would account for the typical bobbing movement of the light. In fact, it is not known what a Hinkypunk looks like from close up, since nobody who has got close to one has ever come back to give a description.

# GRINDYLOW

**A Grindylow is an unpleasant creature that lives in deep ponds and swamps.**

A Grindylow likes to live at the bottom of a deep, still pond or a swamp, preferably somewhere where the surface of the water is covered with weeds so that it's very hard for people to see where the bank ends and the water begins. If you should accidentally step into the water, the Grindylow will grab you with its long skinny arms and drag you down into the depths, where it will probably eat you. The best-known Grindylow is Jenny Greenteeth, who has lived in various marshes in the West of England and is said to be responsible for the disappearance of a number of children.

## GRENDEL AND HIS MOTHER

The Anglo-Saxon poem *Beowulf*, written in the tenth century, tells how the King of the Danes and his people were continually being attacked by Grendel, a giant monster who lived under the swamp. Grendel often attacked when the Danes were feasting, since he hated to hear people singing and having a good time. The brave fighter Beowulf battled with Grendel and finally defeated him, ripping off Grendel's huge arm. But Grendel's mother came looking for revenge, and was even bigger and much, much nastier than her son.

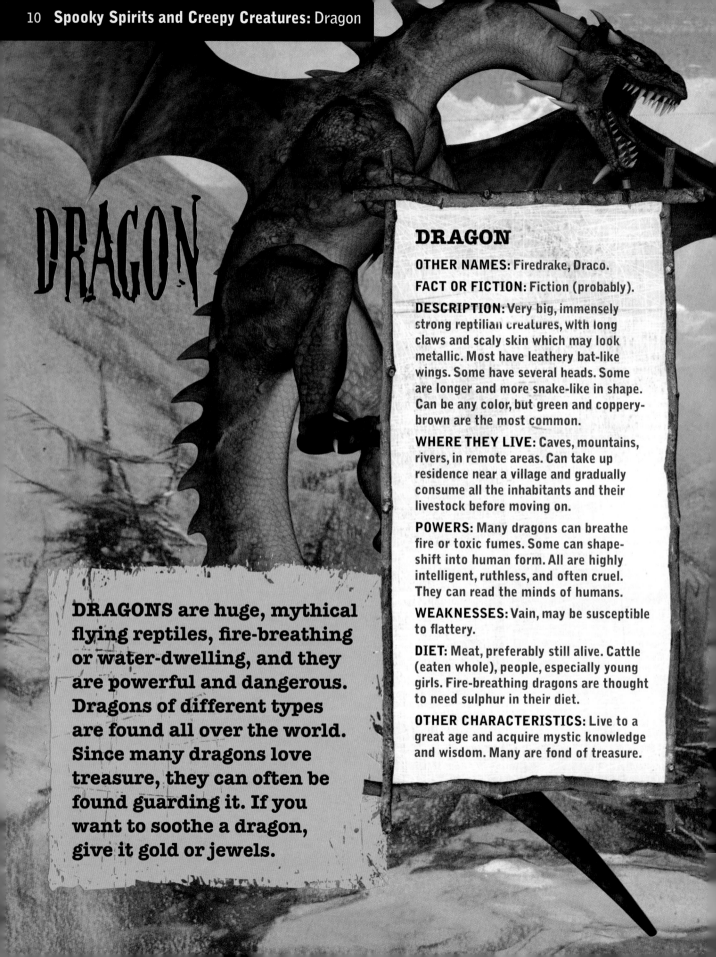

# DRAGON

**DRAGONS** are huge, mythical flying reptiles, fire-breathing or water-dwelling, and they are powerful and dangerous. Dragons of different types are found all over the world. Since many dragons love treasure, they can often be found guarding it. If you want to soothe a dragon, give it gold or jewels.

## DRAGON

**OTHER NAMES:** Firedrake, Draco.

**FACT OR FICTION:** Fiction (probably).

**DESCRIPTION:** Very big, immensely strong reptilian creatures, with long claws and scaly skin which may look metallic. Most have leathery bat-like wings. Some have several heads. Some are longer and more snake-like in shape. Can be any color, but green and coppery-brown are the most common.

**WHERE THEY LIVE:** Caves, mountains, rivers, in remote areas. Can take up residence near a village and gradually consume all the inhabitants and their livestock before moving on.

**POWERS:** Many dragons can breathe fire or toxic fumes. Some can shape-shift into human form. All are highly intelligent, ruthless, and often cruel. They can read the minds of humans.

**WEAKNESSES:** Vain, may be susceptible to flattery.

**DIET:** Meat, preferably still alive. Cattle (eaten whole), people, especially young girls. Fire-breathing dragons are thought to need sulphur in their diet.

**OTHER CHARACTERISTICS:** Live to a great age and acquire mystic knowledge and wisdom. Many are fond of treasure.

## HERE BE DRAGONS

It's often believed that ancient maps used to have the inscription "Here Be Dragons" (in Latin, *hic sunt dracones*) in unexplored areas. In fact, only one known map has this inscription: the Hunt Lenox Globe, which dates from about 1505 AD. The area it marks as dragon-infested is in eastern China.

## TYPES OF DRAGON

Many different descriptions of dragons have come from different countries, but they can all be classified into two main types: fiery dragons and watery dragons.

**Fiery dragons:** These are most often found in western legends and histories. They are the dragons that breathe fire and destroy towns and villages by flying over and scorching them. They're fierce, proud, and cruel, and are the enemies of humans.

**Watery dragons:** These are more common in Asian countries. They're longer and more snaky than the fiery dragons, and are closely linked to water. Sometimes a watery dragon can be the spirit of a river or mountain stream, and will suffer if the stream dries up or is polluted. This type is much kinder to humans, though they still need to be treated with great respect. Watery dragons may appear in human form.

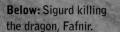

**Below:** Sigurd killing the dragon, Fafnir.

## LEGEND OF FAFNIR

In Scandinavian mythology, Fafnir had to guard a priceless treasure. But he became so obsessed with it that he turned into a greedy and dangerous dragon. He was killed by the hero Sigurd (also known as Siegfried). After being splashed with the dragon's blood, Sigurd finds that he can now understand the language of birds. He hears the birds talking about a plot to kill him, and therefore is able to defeat his enemy.

## DRAGONS AND TREASURE

Fiery dragons are very fond of gold and jewels. Over their long lives, they collect vast amounts of treasure, which they hide in mountain caves. One dragon may take over a treasure when another one dies, so some hoards are very ancient. Dragons are well aware that treasure is attractive to humans, and may use it as bait, allowing unwary thieves to wander into the cave and to gaze in astonishment at the riches on display. The dragon may even chat with them for a while, before eating them. It is unwise to join any expedition to steal a dragon's hoard.

## ASIAN DRAGONS

Dragons are important in Asian culture, especially in China, Vietnam, and Japan.

Here is a list of some Chinese dragons, together with a description of their temperament and powers.

**Shenlong** is a rain dragon with shining blue scales. If annoyed, it can cause thunderstorms and hurricanes.

**Tianlong** is the celestial dragon, another sky-colored Chinese dragon that has power over clouds.

**Fucanglong** is a fiery dragon that mostly lives underground and guards treasure and mineral wealth in the earth. A volcano erupting is thought to be the Fucanglong bursting angrily out of the mountaintop.

**Ch'i** is a mountain dragon, tricky and easily annoyed.

**Jiaolong** is a dragon of floods and rivers. It can shape-shift into a number of different forms including people and fish.

## A VENGEFUL DRAGON

Kiyohime was a pretty young girl who was an innkeeper's daughter. One day she fell madly in love with a young Buddhist priest. However, the priest thought that she wasn't good enough for him because he was educated and she was just a lowly maid. When he rejected her, Kiyohime wanted revenge. She studied magic and learned how to turn herself into a dragon. In her dragon shape, she tracked down the arrogant young man and killed him.

Edente vortich...          sum dolussct impetu scat m

## THE RED DRAGON OF WALES

The national emblem of Wales has always been a red dragon. This goes back to a story about Merlin, the great wizard.

The story tells how a red and a white dragon had been fighting each other and doing terrible damage to the country. They were captured by magic and imprisoned under the hill called Dinas Emrys.

All was quiet then for centuries, until King Vortigern tried to build a castle on the hill. Each day the workmen would start building the walls, and each morning they would find that their work from the day before had been destroyed during the night. Local wise men led Vortigern to a young boy called Merlin, who lived near the hill and who was known to have magic powers. Merlin told the king about the dragons under the hill. Nobody believed him, but finally Vortigern had the hill opened up. Everyone was terrified as the two huge dragons flew out and at once began fighting again. A battle followed, and at last the red dragon overcame and killed the white dragon. This was the beginning of Merlin's career as a great wizard.

**Top:** Battle of the red and white dragons.
**Left:** The red dragon of Wales.

## St. George And The Dragon

St. George, who was originally an ordinary Roman soldier, was once journeying through a desert land when he came to a town where a dragon had taken over the only source of water.

In order to get any water to drink, the people of the town had to give the dragon food to persuade it to move away from the water for a while each day. At first they had fed it with sheep, and then, when the sheep ran out, the dragon had indicated that it would be more cooperative if it was fed with young girls. The girls from the town were being eaten one by one and were drawing lots to see who would go next.

The king's daughter had drawn the fatal lot, and although her father wanted to overrule the result, she insisted that it was her turn and she would go to be eaten like all the other girls. The king had promised all kinds of treasure to anyone who would send their own daughter to the dragon instead, but no one had offered.

Fortunately, at this point St. George arrived. Protecting himself with the sign of the cross, after a hard fight, he killed the dragon with his spear, and the king's daughter was saved.

St. George slays the dragon, saving the king's daughter from a horrible death.

# TROLL

A **TROLL** is a kind of giant, closely connected with stone. Trolls are very stupid but still highly dangerous. They have a close connection with rocks and are often found in caverns deep inside mountains.

## BLOCK HEADS

Trolls are usually very big and grayish in color, with a large head and tiny eyes. In fact, they often look as if they are made from rock. Many Cave Trolls, who live in caverns deep within mountains, can only go outside at night and will actually turn to stone if sunlight touches them.

Most Trolls are extremely stupid and have poor eyesight, but they can still be very dangerous, since they have such huge weight and enormous strength. If a Troll grabs hold of you, you're pretty much done for. Trolls are also very aggressive and will attack for no apparent reason.

Some Trolls are more intelligent and are good at building things. In Scandinavia, Trolls often build bridges and then live under them, like the Troll which tried to eat the Three Billy Goats Gruff in the famous fairytale. This kind of Troll seems to be able to stand sunlight without turning into stone, but is just as mean and aggressive as the other kind. There are many stories of these Trolls deliberately attacking people who are happy and are having a good time.

Ogre

# ORC

### A kind of goblin, very strong and bred for fighting.

Orcs look like short, wide human beings, but they're immensely strong. They're cunning and treacherous. They can endure great hardship, ignore pain, and travel long distances on foot, in a sort of jogging run.

Orcs live only to fight. It's their purpose in life. They were originally bred by an evil magician to be a fighting force. They may do some stealing, bullying, and getting drunk in between fights. They only eat meat, and there have been rumors that they're not too fussy about eating each other.

Orcs were first mentioned in the famous books by J. R. R. Tolkien.

# OGRE

### A very ugly human-eating giant, often covered with hair.

Ogres are usually giants, though they may not be very big, as giants go. However, they make up for that by being extremely ugly—in fact, they are quite hideous to look at. But the main thing about an ogre that makes it truly unpleasant is that it eats people and is always hungry. Fortunately, ogres are not usually very clever so it is quite easy to outwit them if you are smart.

Orc

# Thunderbird

In Native American legend, the Thunderbird is a huge bird with great magical and spiritual powers. The beat of its wings causes the thunder and the lightning flashes from its eyes. In some stories, the Thunderbird is a messenger for the Great Spirit. In other tales, it's more of a trickster spirit and can disguise itself as another creature and even as a human being.

**Left:** The eagle-like Roc.
**Below:** The Native American Thunderbird.

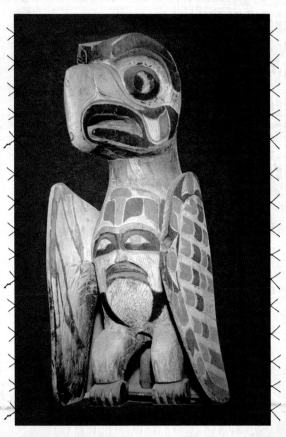

# Roc

The Roc or Rukh is a creature of Arabian legend. It's like an eagle, but enormous—big and powerful enough to prey on elephants. A Roc will seize an elephant in its huge claws and fly up into the air with it. It then drops the elephant from a great height so that it smashes to death, whereupon the Roc flies back down to earth and devours it.

# Ahool

Named after its unnerving cry, the Ahool is a huge bat that is said to fly through the rainforests of Java. It has a face like a monkey and vast leathery wings, with a wingspan of 10 feet (3 m).

# WYVERN

**THE WYVERN is like a small flying dragon. It is a scaly creature with wings and a long, spiked tail. It is more bird-like in shape than a dragon, since it has a beak and only two legs, and its wings are bigger in proportion to its size.**

## FLYING SERPENT

The name "Wyvern" comes from an Anglo-Saxon word for a snake, and there have been tales of Wyverns in Britain and northern Europe for many centuries. Wyverns were believed to be creatures of evil, even messengers of the Devil, and some said that they spread the Plague. Though smaller than dragons—they're sometimes called Dragonets—Wyverns are aggressive and nasty.

Although Wyverns are hard to fight since they are good fliers, the females are supposed to be particularly tricky to deal with.

A rare variation is the Sea Wyvern, which has a fishy tail like that of a mermaid.

The Wyvern was used as a symbol of battle and conquest, and perhaps for this reason, despite being so unpleasant, Wyverns were often used in heraldry as part of a "coat of arms" and are still very popular as symbols, badges, or mascots for sports clubs, towns, schools, etc.

Some cryptozoologists (experts that specialize in animals that are said to exist but haven't been found) think Wyverns might be surviving dinosaurs (pterosaurs) that lived 65 million years ago.

# CHIMERA

**Dreaded by the ancient Greeks, this deadly, fire-breathing creature is three sinister beasts rolled into one.**

A Chimera has the forelegs, shoulders, and head of a lion, the body of a goat with a goat's head on its back, and the tail of a dragon with a serpent's head at its end. The Chimera is thought to have emerged from the mountain of the same name in southwestern Turkey, where, to this day, vents in the ground spout fountains of burning gas. A famous Greek myth tells how a Chimera devastated that region before being killed by the hero Bellephon.

# BASILISK

**Said to be the king of serpents, the Basilisk is a deadly snake with a crown-like crest on its head.**

The Basilisk was first reported in the deserts of Libya in ancient times, and was widely feared in Europe in the Middle Ages. So powerful is its venom that even its breath or hiss is fatal; worse still, it can kill you just by looking at you—in fact, the only way to study one safely is by observing its reflection in a mirror. The weasel is the only creature that can kill a Basilisk, and it does this by using its powerful smell. Strangely, Basilisks are also afraid of chickens, which medieval travelers would often carry for protection in Basilisk-infested realms.

# COCKATRICE

**The fearsome dragon-like Cockatrice is often confused with the Basilisk, and some say it is the same creature.**

Like the Basilisk, the Cockatrice can kill with just a bite or a look. But although it has the tail of a serpent, the Cockatrice has the head of a rooster, several legs, and strong wings. And, whereas a Basilisk is born when a rooster incubates the egg of a serpent or toad, a Cockatrice is brought to life when a toad or serpent hatches the egg of a rooster.

**Below:** The Cockatrice is similar to the Basilisk but it has legs and the head of a rooster.

# AMPHISBAENA

**With a head and poisonous fangs at either end of its body, this venomous snake spells double trouble.**

Native to the deserts of North Africa, the Amphisbaena is said to have been born from the spilled blood of the famous snake-haired Gorgon of Greek mythology, Medusa. In medieval imagery, it is sometimes depicted with a lizard-like body, the legs of a chicken, and feathered wings. Though dangerous, it is believed to have medicinal benefits: wearing an Amphisbaena skin around your neck might not look or smell great, but it is said to cure arthritis and the common cold.

## GREMLIN

### A destructive imp that specializes in damaging aircraft.

Probably a relative of the Boggart and the Poltergeist, the Gremlin loves to cause damage to machinery. It particularly likes to sabotage aircraft, and, in fact, pilots in the British Royal Air Force were the first to establish the existence of Gremlins. They suspected that repeated damage to aircraft couldn't just be chalked up to bad luck or a careless mechanic—something was actually sabotaging their planes. Seeing toothmarks on frayed cables really made them wonder!

## MOTHMAN

### A flying man who is a harbinger of doom.

The Mothman was seen by a number of people in Point Pleasant, West Virginia, in 1966–67, and, according to some reports, has been seen occasionally since then. He is described as 7 feet (2.1 m) tall with red, glowing eyes and huge wings, with a wingspan of maybe 10 feet (3 m).

Although the Mothman will not hurt you, seeing him is a sign that something very bad is going to happen, and anyone who sees him gains an extra ability to foretell what the upcoming bad event will be.

There is a convincing theory that the Mothman is actually just a large heron, but Point Pleasant celebrates him with an annual Mothman Festival every September.

# GRIFFIN

**A majestic and ferocious mythical beast, half lion and half eagle.**

The Griffin, or Gryphon, has the body, back legs, and tail of a lion and the head, front legs, and wings of an eagle. It also has little pointed ears, but these are the only charming things about a Griffin, which is a big scary monster built for battle and destruction. It has long talons on its eagle-type front feet and a huge sharp beak, plus all the strength of a lion. Do not, on any account, annoy a Griffin.

For some reason, Griffins hate horses, and horses feel the same about Griffins. Given the chance, a Griffin will kill and eat any horse it happens to meet.

On the other hand, Griffins love gold, which they collect and hoard.

# HIPPOGRIFF

**A cross between a Griffin and a horse.**

Strangely, given that Griffins hate horses, the two beasts are the parents of the Hippogriff (also spelled Hippogryph). This legendary monster has the eagle head and wings of a Griffin, a lion-like body, and the back legs of a horse. Not surprisingly, Hippogriffs have a reputation for being crazy, wild, and treacherous. Because of the hostility between horses and Griffins, Hippogriffs are also very, very rare.

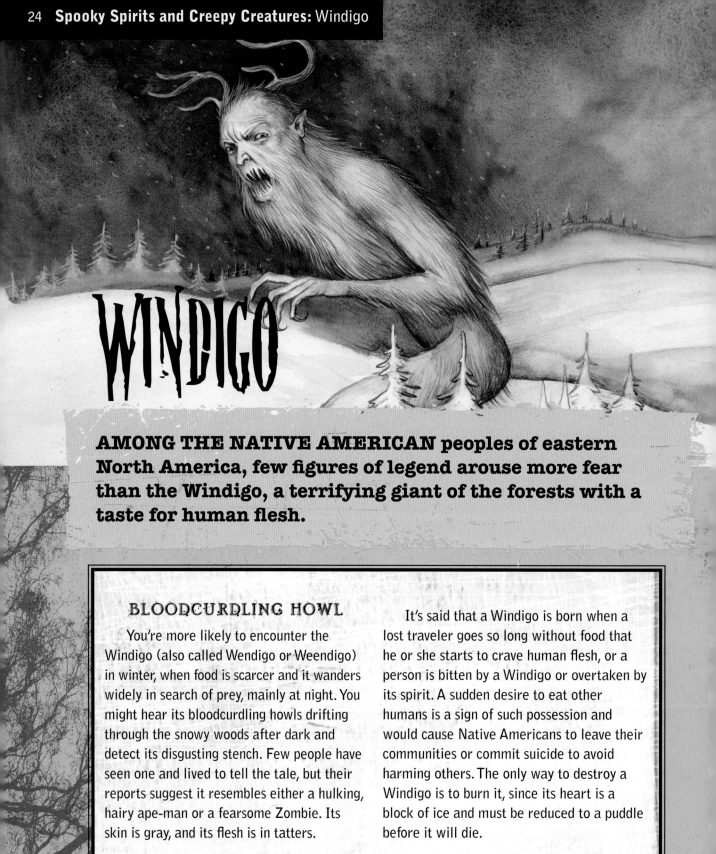

# WINDIGO

**AMONG THE NATIVE AMERICAN** peoples of eastern North America, few figures of legend arouse more fear than the Windigo, a terrifying giant of the forests with a taste for human flesh.

### BLOODCURDLING HOWL

You're more likely to encounter the Windigo (also called Wendigo or Weendigo) in winter, when food is scarcer and it wanders widely in search of prey, mainly at night. You might hear its bloodcurdling howls drifting through the snowy woods after dark and detect its disgusting stench. Few people have seen one and lived to tell the tale, but their reports suggest it resembles either a hulking, hairy ape-man or a fearsome Zombie. Its skin is gray, and its flesh is in tatters.

It's said that a Windigo is born when a lost traveler goes so long without food that he or she starts to crave human flesh, or a person is bitten by a Windigo or overtaken by its spirit. A sudden desire to eat other humans is a sign of such possession and would cause Native Americans to leave their communities or commit suicide to avoid harming others. The only way to destroy a Windigo is to burn it, since its heart is a block of ice and must be reduced to a puddle before it will die.

# MNGWA

Many fearless hunters who regularly track down lions and leopards in Tanzania, east Africa, live in terror of the Mngwa, or "strange one," a giant cat bigger than a lion or a leopard and even fiercer. Said to be as large as a donkey and have thick, gray, striped fur, it is mentioned in old African songs and was reported to have claimed several human victims in the 1920s and 1930s. The victims, who had been totally mutilated, were said to be clutching gray hairs in their dead hands. Europeans who heard the stories of the Mngwa assumed that it might be a dragon, rather than a cat-like creature. There have been many unsuccessful attempts to hunt and kill the Mngwa.

# BOKWUS

If you stroll through a spruce forest in northwestern North America and catch sight of a painted face peering at you through the trees, beware. For it could be a Bokwus, an evil spirit of Native American lore that hunts human souls. Its favorite trick is to sneak up on people fishing and thrust them under the water to drown them.

# ASANBOSAM

In the forests of Ghana, Côte d'Ivoire, and Togo in west Africa, danger may lurk on high. Humanlike vampires called Asanbosams are said to hang from branches by hooks at the ends of their legs, ready to snatch up or drop onto passersby and tear at their throats with teeth made of iron. The mere mention of the name is supposed to bring bad luck— so never say it out loud!

Medusa, one of the three Gorgon sisters.

# GORGON

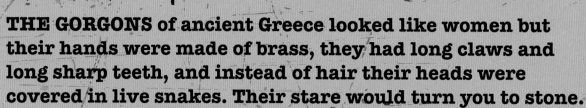

**THE GORGONS** of ancient Greece looked like women but their hands were made of brass, they had long claws and long sharp teeth, and instead of hair their heads were covered in live snakes. Their stare would turn you to stone.

## SERPENTINE SISTERS

The Gorgons were three sisters: Stheno, Euryale, and Medusa. Stheno and Euryale were immortal, but Medusa, the youngest, was mortal. The Greek hero Perseus succeeded in killing Medusa, with the help of several gods (Hermes lent him winged sandals, Hades lent him a hat of invisibility, and Athena lent him a brightly polished shield). Moving swiftly in the sandals and unseen by Medusa because of the hat, Perseus was able to use the shield like a mirror and see where the Gorgon was without looking at her directly, so he could kill her without being turned to stone. He cut off her head, which lost none of its power. He used it to defeat several enemies before he presented it to the goddess Athena, who kept it on her shield.

PERSEUS SHOWING THE GORGON'S HEAD.

# Buru Buru

The Buru Buru is a legendary giant lizard in the remote valleys of the Himalayas. It is bigger than a Komodo dragon, which is the biggest lizard known to science. The Buru Buru is over 20 feet (6 m) long. It is dark blue in color and has three rows of spines down its back. Not much is known about its character or habits, but if it's anything like the Komodo dragon, they will be pretty unpleasant.

# Minhocão

The Minhocão is like a huge black version of a garden earthworm: some reports have described it as 80 feet (25 m) long, with two tentacles or stalks on its head—these may be its eyes, like those of a snail. It is so powerful that it can uproot whole trees in its path and is covered with bones that create a kind of armor for its body. It is said to burrow through the earth in unexplored parts of highlands in South America.

**Right:** The Buru Buru resembles the Komodo dragon.

# Tazelwurm

The Tazelwurm, or "worm with feet," has been sighted in the Swiss, Bavarian, and Austrian Alps. It is described as whitish and lizard-like but smooth-skinned and not scaly. Its head is shaped more like that of a cat, and the worm is about 8 feet (2.5 m) long. Its bite is poisononous, it leaps well, and pounces on its prey. It protects itself by having tough skin that a sword cannot penetrate. If a Tazelwurm is injured, you'll see its green blood. It is also known as Bergstutzen ("mountain stump"), Springewurm ("jumping worm"), or Stollenwurm ("tunnel worm").

# GLOSSARY

**Ancient:** of or relating to a period of time long past

**Anglo-Saxon:** of English ancestry

**Cavern:** a cave often of large or unknown size

**Celestial:** of or relating to the sky

**Changeling:** a child secretly exchanged for another in infancy

**Cryptozoologist:** expert that specializes in animals that are said to exist but haven't been found

**Drawing lots:** to choose an object to determine an answer by chance

**Emblem:** a device, symbol, design, or figure used as an identifying mark

**Immortal:** living forever

**Inscription:** something that has been written, engraved, or printed on

**Livestock:** animals that are kept or raised

**Medieval:** of or relating to the Middle Ages

**Mythical:** existing only in the imagination

**Plague:** a disease that affects many people and causes a high rate of death

**Prey:** an animal hunted or killed by another animal for food

**Rogue:** a dishonest or wicked person

**Sulphur:** a nonmetallic element that occurs either free or combined especially in sulfides and sulfates

**Supernatural:** of or relating to an existence of something beyond the observable universe

**Treacherous:** likely to betray

# INDEX

Please visit our website, www.garethstevens.com. For a free color catalog of all our high-quality books, call toll free 1-800-542-2595 or fax 1-877-542-2596.

Library of Congress Cataloging-in-Publication Data

Cox, Barbara.
Spooky spirits and creepy creatures / by Barbara Cox and Scott Forbes.
  p. cm. — (Creepy chronicles)
Includes index.
ISBN 978-1-4824-0245-2 (phk )
ISBN 978-1-4824-0246-9 (6-pack)
ISBN 978-1-4824-0243-8 (library binding)
1.Spirits — Juvenile literature. 2.  Monsters — Juvenile literature. 3. Supernatural — Juvenile literature. I. Title.
BF1461.C69 2014
133.1—dc23

First Edition

Published in 2014 by
**Gareth Stevens Publishing**
111 East 14th Street, Suite 349
New York, NY 10003

Produced for Gareth Stevens by Red Lemon Press Limited
Concept and Project Manager: Ariana Klepac
Designer: Emilia Toia
Design Assistant: Haylee Bruce
Picture Researcher: Ariana Klepac
Text: Scott Forbes (Forest, Castle, Desert), Barbara Cox (all other text)
Indexer: Trevor Matthews

Images: Every effort has been made to trace and contact the copyright holders prior to publication. If notified, the publisher undertakes to rectify any errors or omissions at the earliest opportunity.

Bridgeman Art Library: 2 tl and b, 3 tr, 6 tl in box (Fairy Art Museum, Tokyo, Japan) and br, 7 tl, 8 t, 9 br in box, 10–11 background, 12 cl, 14 t (Lambeth Palace Library, London), 14–15 background, 15 b, 16–17 background, cover and 16 t (National Museum, Stockholm, Sweden), 17 tl, 22 br, 23 tl, 20 b, 21 b.
iStockphoto: other images as follows:
cross stitches 6, 8, 12; grunge borders 9, 13, 15; hands 9, 13, 15; stick borders 10, mountain landscape 12–13; butterfly 22;
Martin Hargreaves: 23 tr, 24 t, 9 t.

Shutterstock: all other images


KEY: t = top, b = bottom, l = left, r = right, c = center

Printed in the United States of America

CPSIA compliance information: Batch #CW14GS: For further information contact Gareth Stevens, New York, New York at 1-800-542-2595.

Gareth Stevens
Publishing